Anglais

Cycle 3 / CM1

Cup of Tea

Gisèle ALBAGNAC
Conseillère pédagogique
chargée des langues

Randolph BOYD
Intervenant anglais
en classe élémentaire

hachette ÉDUCATION

Micro-Climate est une association que nous avons créée, destinée à promouvoir l'enseignement de l'anglais au travers de méthodes actives. Toutes nos productions ont fait l'objet d'expérimentations au quotidien dans des classes élémentaires et dans des stages de vacances destinés aux enfants de cycle 3.

Gisèle Albagnac et Randolph Boyd

Responsable éditoriale : Stéphanie-Paule SAÏSSE
Éditeur assistant : Marie LUCAS

Création de maquette de couverture : Laurent CARRÉ
Illustrations de la couverture : Jérôme BRASSEUR, Camille LADOUSSE et Alain BOYER
Exécution de la maquette de couverture : TYPOVIRGULE

Création de maquette intérieure : Delphine d'INGUIMBERT et Valérie GOUSSOT
Mise en pages : Delphine d'INGUIMBERT et Valérie GOUSSOT
Illustrations : Camille LADOUSSE
Cartes et dessins techniques (pages 9, 16, 30, 31, 32, 58, 65, 72 et 74) **:** Nathalie GUÉVENEUX
Recherche iconographique : Marie LUCAS

ISBN : 978-2-01-117353-9

PRÉFACE

Apprendre une langue, c'est être capable de prendre des informations dans tout ce que tu entends, tout ce que tu vois, d'utiliser en fait tous tes sens et tes connaissances pour comprendre ce qui se passe autour de toi.

Tu dois être capable de lire l'expression d'un visage, d'interpréter un geste, de mettre du sens dans une intonation pour réellement entrer dans une situation de communication.

C'est dans cet esprit que nous avons écrit ***Cup of Tea***.

Nous te proposons de découvrir l'anglais par le biais de l'oral. Dans chaque séance, tu écouteras une saynète. Tu pourras émettre des hypothèses sur ce que tu penses avoir compris, tu pourras ensuite t'aider des illustrations de ton livre pour les confirmer, répéter certains passages ou mots-clés et te mettre en situation en mimant la scène.

Les activités t'aideront à comprendre et à retenir le vocabulaire de la séance.

Dans chaque unité, une double page « Power Action » te permettra de pratiquer des situations en lien avec les autres disciplines (mathématiques, histoire, géographie, sciences, arts plastiques…).

Pour que tu puisses découvrir une culture nouvelle, nous avons introduit des pages « Civilization » pour te permettre de mieux connaître les modes de vie et la civilisation anglophones.

Enfin, pour te familiariser avec le rythme et l'intonation de l'anglais, tu pourras écouter, lire et répéter les chansons que nous avons écrites pour toi.

Et maintenant, tu as soif d'apprendre l'anglais ? Rejoins Serena, David, Wayne et Griff pour une ***cup of tea***…

Les auteurs

SUMMARY

SUMMARY

Unit 4

Unit 5

INTRODUCTION

Discovery

▶ Look at your teacher and listen.

▶ Listen and point.

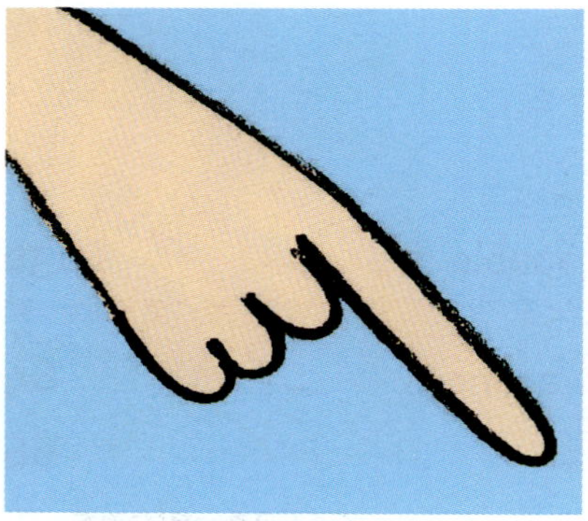

Point

Look

Speak

Act

Listen

Put your hand up

▶ Listen and repeat.

▶ Look at your teacher, act and speak.

You know some English!

- Listen.

- Listen and point.

a tent

a train

a lamp

an envelope

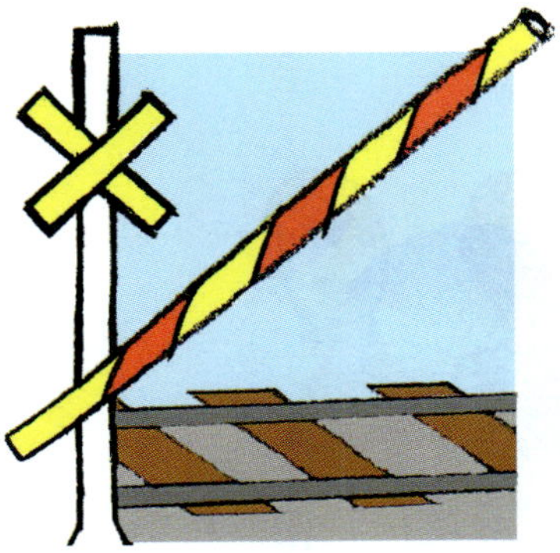
a barrier

a panda

an orange

a rose

- Listen and repeat.

- Look at the words.
  - Any remarks?

- Listen and discuss with your teacher.

Unit 1 HELLO! WHO ARE YOU?

- Listen.
- Look and listen.

- Listen and repeat.
- Act and speak (work in pairs).
  - Who are you?

1 Listen to the chant

I am David.
I come from Cardiff.
I say hello,
You say goodbye.
I say hello,
Good morning,
Good afternoon,
Good evening.
Uh huh...
Oh yeaaa...
And who are you?

2 Do it yourself

I am ...
I come from ...
I say ...,
You say ...
I say ...,
Good ...,
Good ...,
Good ...
Uh huh...
Oh yeaaa...
And who are you?

3 The world around me

- Listen.
- Listen and point.

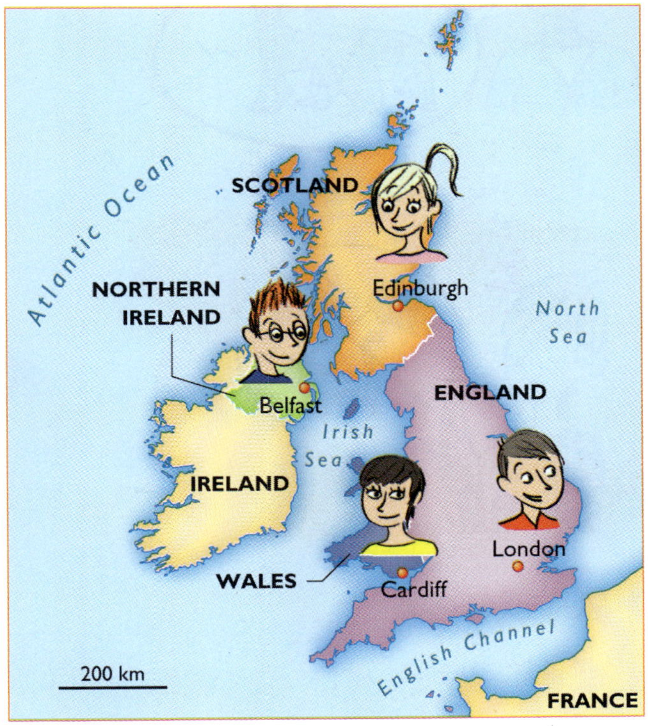

Remember

Good morning	Good afternoon
Good evening	Goodbye
Who are you?	I am (David).
I come from (Cardiff).	

SOUNDS [I] listen or [i:] teacher

- Listen and repeat.
- Listen and put your hand up when you hear [i:].

HAVE YOU GOT A PET?

▶ Listen.

▶ Look and listen.

▶ Listen and repeat.

▶ Listen, repeat and point.

1 Listen to the chant

A cat and a mouse
Dancing in a house
Not really! Not really!

A big grey rabbit
Swimming with a goldfish
Not really! Not really!

A dog and a hamster
Going to Manchester
Not really! Not really!
And why not?

2 Do it yourself

A ... and a ...
...
Not really! Not really!

A ... and a ...
...
Not really! Not really!

A ... and a ...
...
Not really! Not really!
And why not?

3 The world around me: a survey

- Copy and complete.

Ask your friends: "have you got a pet?" (groups of five).

Name	....	....	....	....	....	....
Pets	....	....	....	....	....	....
Total	....	....	....	....	....	....

4 Let's find out

- Is it a pet? Listen, point and speak.
- Now test your friend.

Remember

- **Have you got (a pet)? Yes, I have / No, I haven't.**
- **I have got (a pet). / I haven't got (a pet).**
- **a goldfish, a mouse, a dog, a guinea pig, a rabbit, a cat, a hamster.**

SOUNDS [k] cat or [g] goldfish

- Listen and repeat.
- Listen and put your hand up when you hear [g].

WHO IS THIS?

▶ Listen.

▶ Look and listen.

▶ Listen, repeat and point with Serena.

1 Listen to the chant

Tic toc tic tic toc
Visit grandpa
Visit grandma

Tic toc tic tic toc
Visit uncle
Visit aunty

Tic toc tic tic toc
Play with cousins
Go home to see
Father, mother,
Sister, brother,
Can I have a cup of tea?

2 He or she?

- Listen and put your hand up.

- Now create your own questions and ask your friends.

3 Let's find out (work in pairs)

- Ask your friend: "have you got brothers and sisters?".
- If yes, introduce them to the class.

4 Guessing game

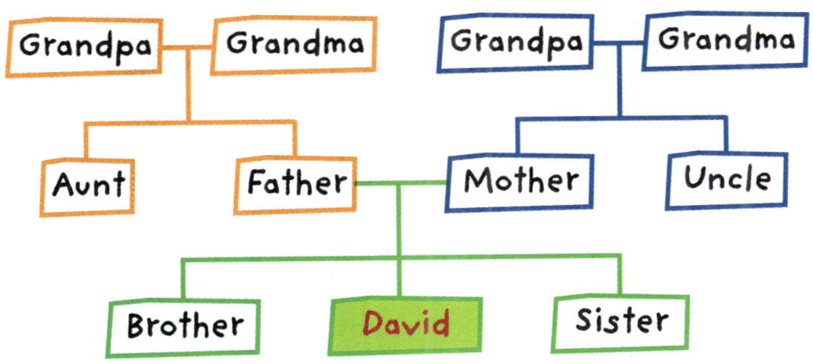

- Listen and put your hand up.
- The brother of my father is my uncle!
- The sister of my mother is my ....
- The father of my mother is my ....
- My uncle and my aunty have got two children: they are my ....
- The mother of my father is my ....

Remember

- Who is this?
- What's your brother's name?
- father, mother, brother, sister, grandpa, grandma, uncle, aunt(y), cousin.

SOUNDS

[ð] weather or [θ] birthday

- Listen and repeat.
- Listen and put your hand up when you hear [θ].

4 Unit 1 WHEN IS YOUR BIRTHDAY?

▶ Listen.

▶ Look and listen.

▶ Listen and repeat.

▶ Act and speak (work in pairs).

- Call a friend for his or her birthday.

1 Listen to the chant

My birthday, the day I was born
Your birthday, the day you were born
Happy birthday once a year
It's my birthday, give three cheers:
Hip hip hooray!
Hip hip hooray!
Hip hip hooray!

2 Let's find out

- Right or wrong?

Eight plus two equals ten.
→ Right!
Ten minus three equals eight.
→ Wrong... Seven!

- Six plus three equals nine.
- Seven minus one equals five.
- Nine minus five equals four.
- Two plus two plus three equals eight.
- Two plus seven minus five equals one.

- Now test your friends.

3 The world around me: a survey.

- Copy and complete.

Ask your friends: "when's your birthday?" (groups of five).

Month	January	February	March	April	May	June
Names	....	....	....	....	....	....
Month	**July**	**August**	**September**	**October**	**November**	**December**
Names	....	....	....	....	....	....
Total	....	....	....	....	....	....

Remember

How old are you? — **I am nine (years old).**
How old is she / he? — **She / He is ten.**
When is your birthday? — **My birthday is in June.**
Hip hip hooray!

SOUNDS [b] book or [p] please

- Listen and repeat.
- Listen and put your hand up when you hear [p].

Power... action!

1 How well do you know the United Kingdom?

- Use tracing paper to copy the map.

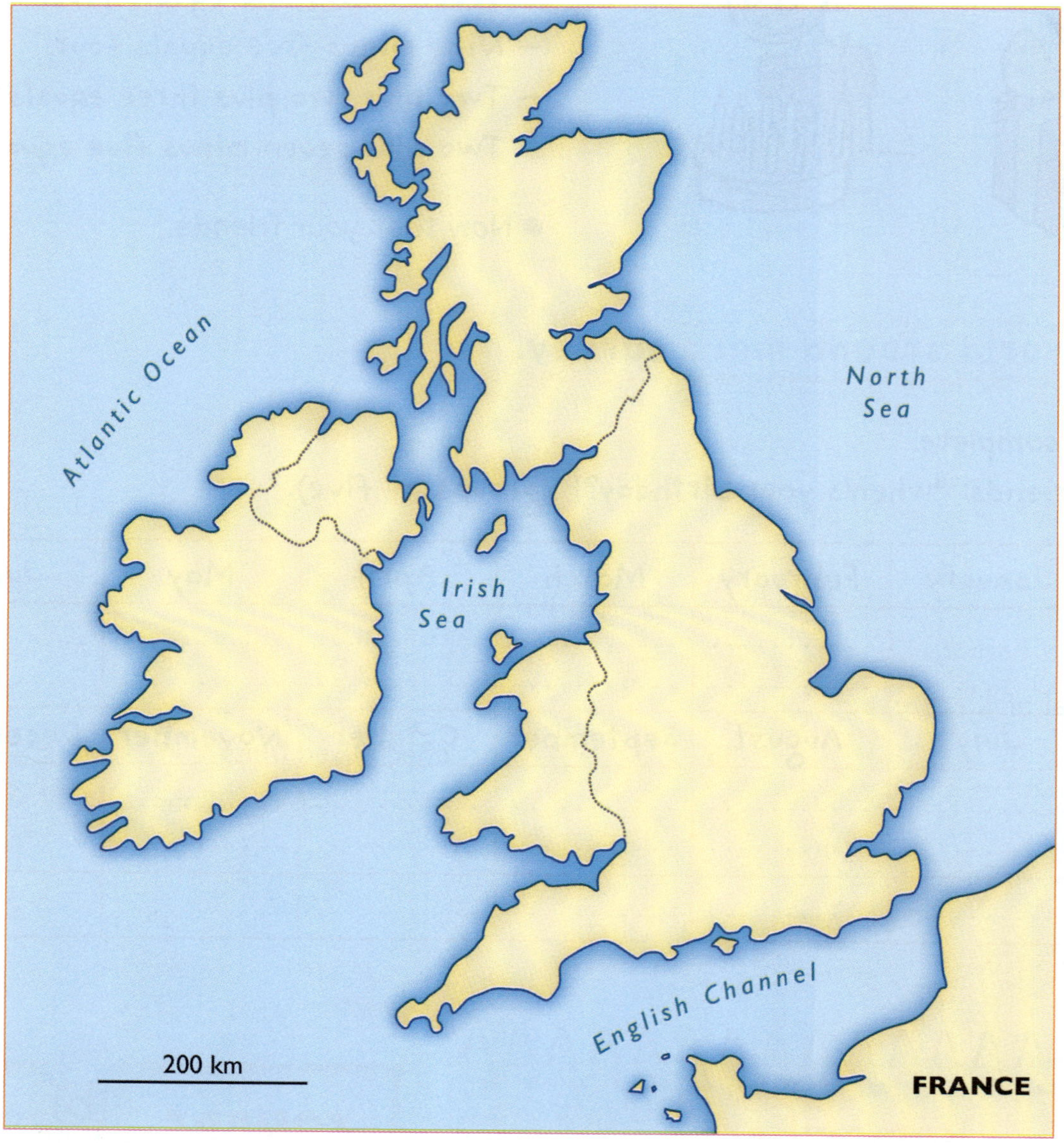

- Using an atlas, colour:

– England in **red**;

– Scotland in **violet**;

– Wales in **green**;

– Northern Ireland in **yellow**.

- Write the names of the different territories.

2 A London tour with Simon

- **Play the game "Simon says" with your teacher.**

Simon says: "Mime a cat".

Simon says: "Touch something blue".

"Form groups of four".

...

Get on

- **Listen to the problem.**
Only do what Simon says!

- **How many passengers will finish the tour with Simon?**

Get off

Workshop

- **Let's make a bread pudding for Serena's birthday.**
- **Ingredients:**

– 1 loaf of white bread

– 1 packet of mixed spices

– Sugar to taste

– A small packet of margarine (125 gr.)

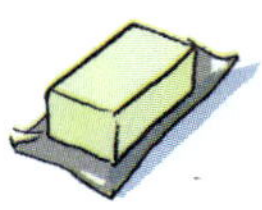

– 3 yoghurt pots of dried mixed fruits

– 2 table spoons of flour

– 1 egg

– 1 small bottle of vanilla essence

- **How to make it:**

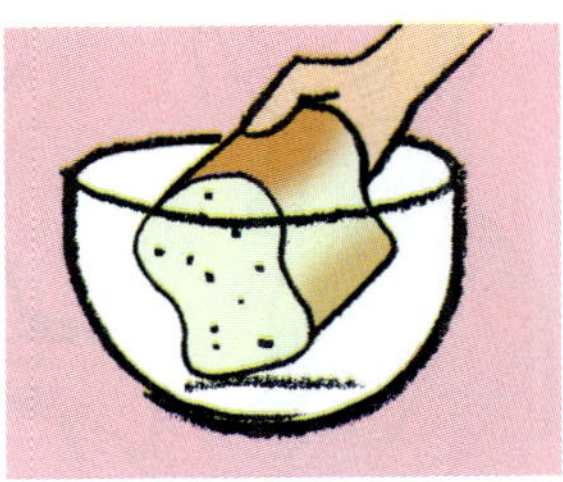

Put the bread in a bowl.

Cover it in cold water.

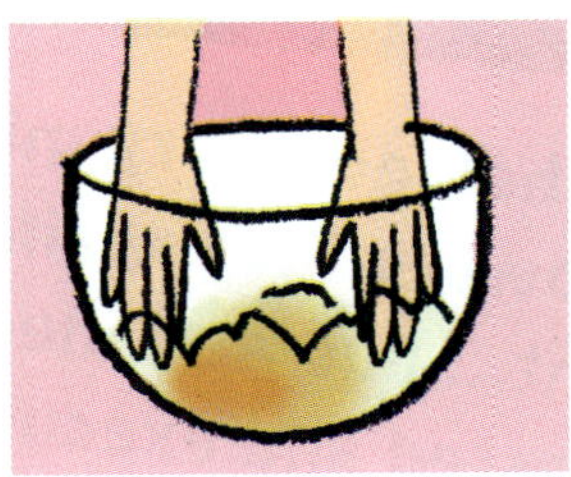

Mix all the ingredients together.

Cook in a baking tray for 90 minutes at medium temperature.

GUY FAWK

Welcome to Bonfire Night!

Come on, everybody!
The country is burning!
Fire, fire!
Fire, fire!
Firemen, fetch the engines!
Come on, everybody!
The country is burning!

My name is Guy Fawkes, I was born in 1570.

In 1605, I helped to organize the Gunpowder Plot against Parliament... but we failed and I was arrested and executed.

ES' NIGHT

Today English people remember me and celebrate with bonfires and fireworks!

"REMEMBER, REMEMBER THE 5th OF NOVEMBER"

Children make manikins representing me and ask for "a penny for the Guy".

Then they burn me on bonfires. It's hot... Just play it cool!

Sing a song

WHO ARE YOU?

Who are you?
On me you know
You can depend,
Together we play
Together we'll stay.
On me you know
You can depend,
I'm your friend,
Your very best friend.

Who are you?
With me you learn
To read and write,
With me you learn
What's wrong or right.
With me you learn
To read and write,
I'm your teacher,
Can't you see?

Who are you?
I am the one
Who makes your bed,
I am the one
Who cries for you.
I am the one
Who makes your bed,
I'm your mother,
I love you.

Written by Micro-Climate

Evaluation ▸ Unit 1

1 Hello! who are you?

- A girl from England meets a boy from Wales. Create a dialogue.

2 Have you got a pet?

- Name the pets you know.

3 Who is this?

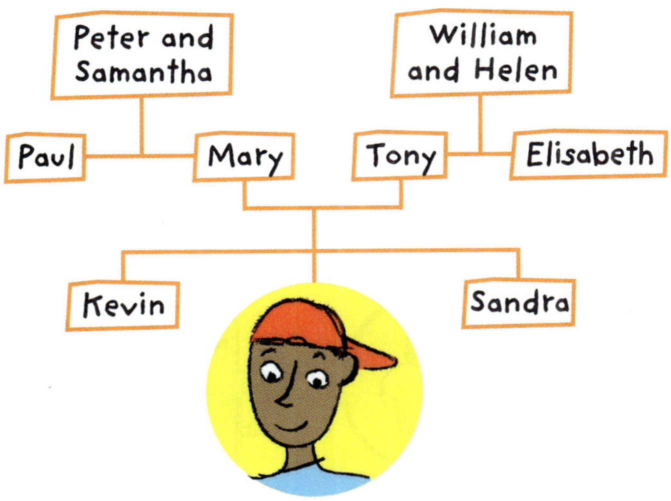

- Look at this family tree and speak about Wayne's family.

4 When is your birthday?

- Peter rings Rebecca about her birthday. Create the conversation.

Unit 2 — 1 GET UP!

▶ Listen.

▶ Look and listen.

▶ Listen, repeat and point.

▶ Act and speak (work in pairs).

- What would you like for breakfast?

1 Listen to the chant

Put on your shirt, Burt!
Hurry up!
Put on your jumper, Peter!
Hurry up!
Put on your hat, Pat!
Hurry up!
Put on your coat,
Your scarf,
Your socks,
Your shoes,
Hurry up!
No pyjamas!
No pyjamas!

2 Do it yourself

It's cold today.
What shall I wear?
..., ...,
..., ...,
Let's hurry up!
Let's hurry up!

It's hot today.
...
..., ...,
..., ...,
Let's ...
...

3 Let's find out

- What shall I put on?
Listen, point and repeat.
- Now describe what your friend is wearing today.

Remember

Get up!	Hurry up!
What shall I put on?	What shall I wear?
What would you like ...?	I would like ...
You are late.	

SOUNDS [t] late or [d] David

- Listen
and repeat.
- Listen and put your hand up when you hear [d].

2 Unit 2 HOW DO YOU SPELL IT?

▶ Listen.

▶ Look and listen.

▶ Listen, repeat and point.

▶ Listen and repeat the alphabet.

A B C D E F G H I J K L M

N O P Q R S T U V W X Y Z

1 Listen to the song

A B C D
E F G
H I J K
L M N O
K L M N O P Q
K L M N O P Q
Q R S T U V
W X Y and Z

2 Let's find out (work in pairs)

- How do you spell it? Put your school things in order.

- Now prepare your own words and ask your friend.

3 The world around me (work in pairs)

- Listen, point and repeat.
- Now spell the name of each item to your friend.

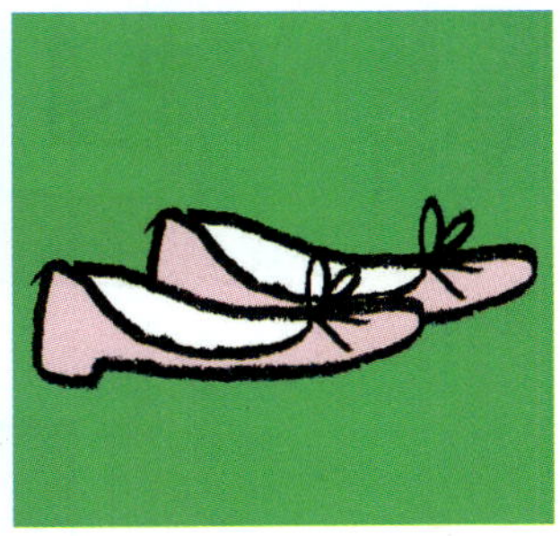

Remember

- the alphabet
- school things: a school bag, a pencil case, a pen, a pencil, a rubber, a ruler, scissors, felt markers

SOUNDS

[ʊ] look or [u:] shoe

- Listen and repeat.
- Listen and put your hand up when you hear [ʊ].

3 HOW ARE YOU?

Unit 2

▶ Listen.

▶ Look and listen.

▶ Listen and repeat.

▶ Act and speak (work in pairs).

- You meet a friend on your way to school. Create a dialogue.

1 Listen to the chant

History, Math, French and Geography,
What a sad day!
What a sad day!
Why? Because!
I'm not good at it!

Art, Science, English and Sport,
What a cool day!
What a cool day!
Why? Because!
Because I'm good at it!

2 Let's find out

(work in pairs)

- Ask your friends:
"what lesson do you like?".

3 The world around me (work in groups)

- Copy and complete your timetable in English.

	Monday	Tuesday	Wednesday	Thursday	Friday	Saturday
Morning	....	....	....	....	....	....
Afternoon	....	....	....	....	....	....

4 How are you?

- Listen and point.

Remember

How are you?
Not so good.
I'm (not) good at maths.
What's up?
Why? Because ...

SOUNDS

[w]
warm

- Listen and repeat.

TONGUE TWISTER

William wears a wonderful red waistcoat.

4 Unit 2 LET'S HAVE SOME ART

▶ Listen.

▶ Look and listen.

▶ Listen and repeat.

▶ Listen, repeat and point.

1 Listen to the chant

Come back, Jack!
Go on, Ron!
Be glad, Brad!
Let's sing the song the same old way!

Come on, John!
Relax, Max!
Good boy, Roy!
Let's do the dance the same old way!

More red, Ted!
Some grey, May!
More blue, Andrew!
Let's paint the world the same old way!

2 Guessing game

- Listen and point.

- Now draw your own artist and describe him or her.

3 The world around me

- Describe the people on these paintings.

The painter's daughters chasing a butterfly,
Thomas Gainsborough
(1759).

An old man and his dog seated by a road,
Sir Edwin Landseer
(19th century).

Remember

- **He is tall. / He's tall.**
- **She is small. / She's small.**
- **big, small, tall, slim, fat, young, old, beautiful.**

SOUNDS [æ] Dad or [ɑ:] guitar

- Listen and repeat.
- Listen and put your hand up when you hear [ɑ:].

Power... action!

1 Let's have some geometry

- Follow the instructions to draw a geometrical design.

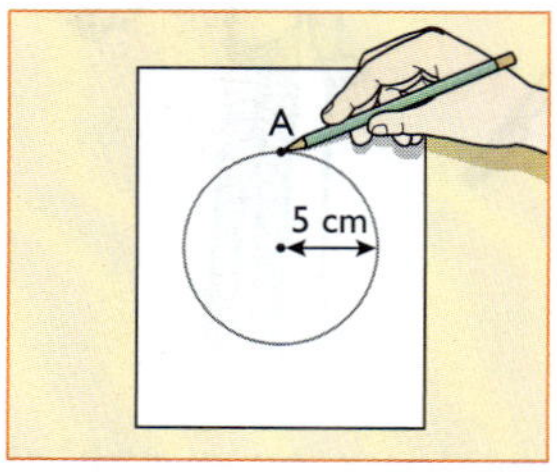

With your compass, draw a circle with a 5 cm radius. Mark a point on the circle and call it "A".

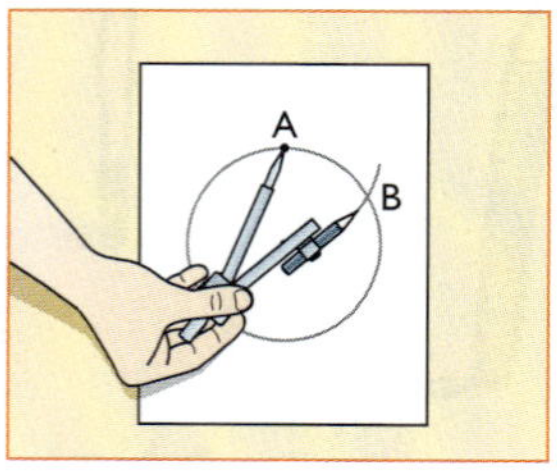

Put the point of the compass on the mark called "A". Keeping the same distance, mark the circle again (point "B").

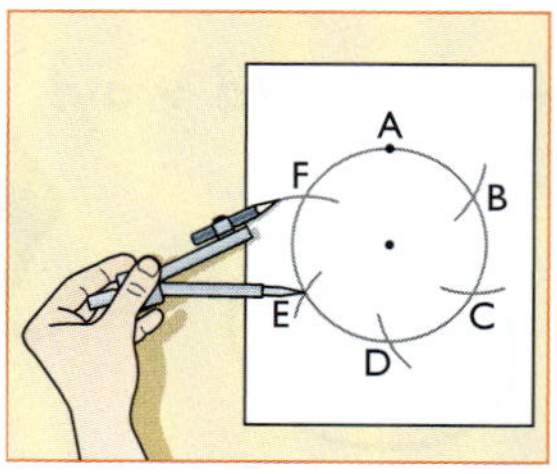

Repeat the action for C, D, E, F.

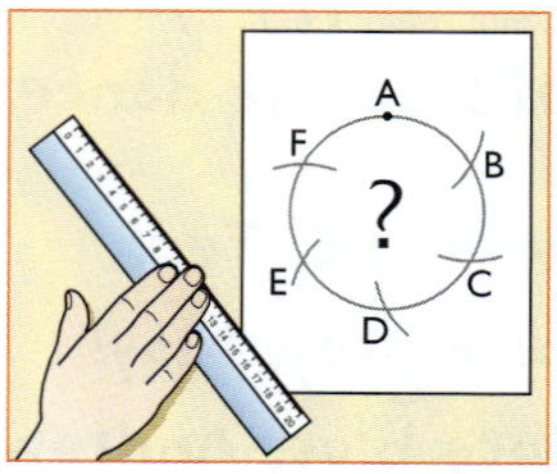

With a ruler, join A to C, C to E, E to A, B to D, D to F, F to B.
What can you see?

2 A statue and an artist

- Describe this statue.
- On the Internet, look for other statues by Niki de Saint-Phalle and information about her.
- Draw a character in the same style and describe it.

A sculpture by
Niki de Saint-Phalle.

3 A skipping game
(a game to play outside)

- Look, listen and then play.

Workshop

- Let's make a Robin Hood hat.
- What you need:
  - – scissors 
  - – an A3 green sheet of rigid paper 
  - – glue 
  - – red paper to make feathers 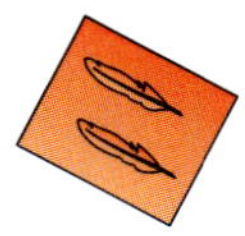
- How to make it:

Fold the sheet in 2

Fold the 2 top corners bringing them to the middle.

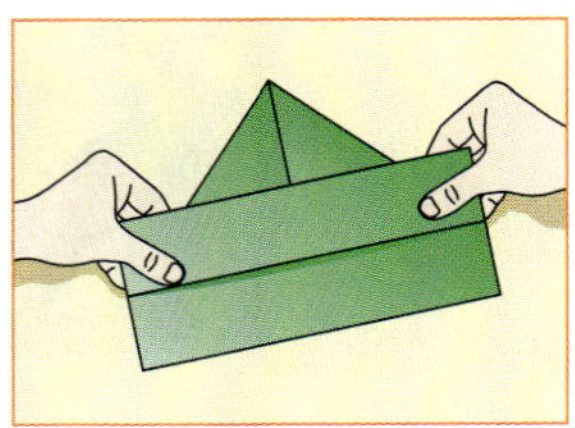

Fold the 2 flaps, one on each side.

Fold ers on each side. e hat.

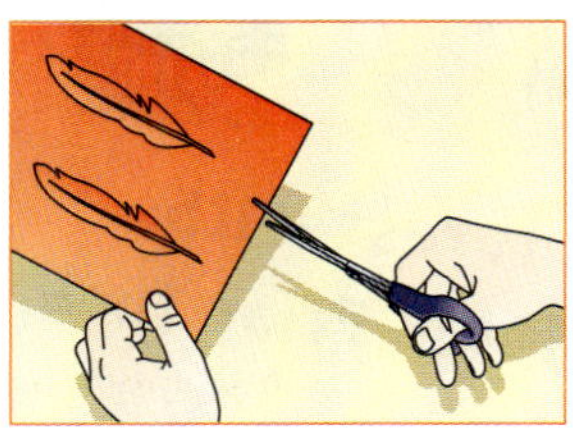

With the red paper, make some feathers.

Stick the feathers on the hat.

Robin

Welcome to Sherwood forest!

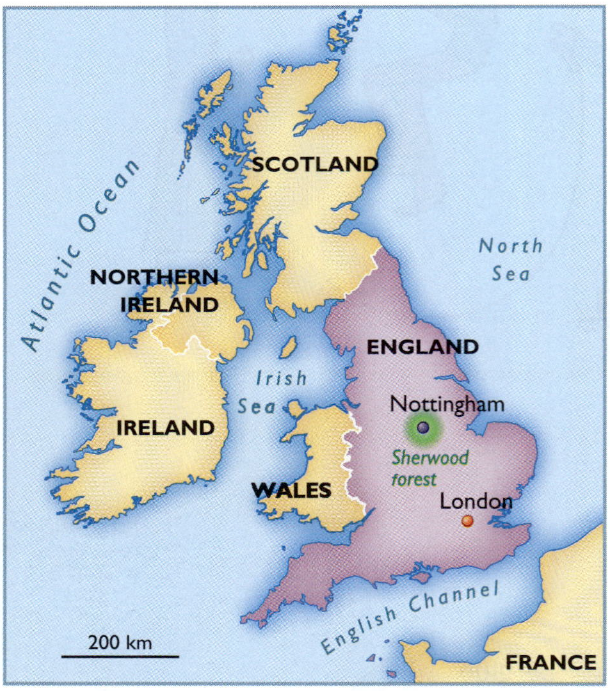

My name is Robin of Loxley... But everyone knows me as Robin Hood!

I live in Sherwood forest with my friends: Little John, Friar Tuck, Will Scarlett...

Hood

The legend says I robbed from the rich to help the poor.

Your money or your life!

© Disney

I am still very famous today!

Books and films tell my story!

Sing a song

Numbers

One is always the beginning,
A figure on its own.
To the sporting it's true,
It's better to have won.

Two is a couple,
Can even be a pair.
To make it supple to divide,
The other must be there.

Numbers can be many things:
Lottery, history...
But if I am your number one,
When all is said and done,
Together we are one.

Three is a trio,
A trio playing jazz.
Four is North, South, East and
West,
What about the rest?

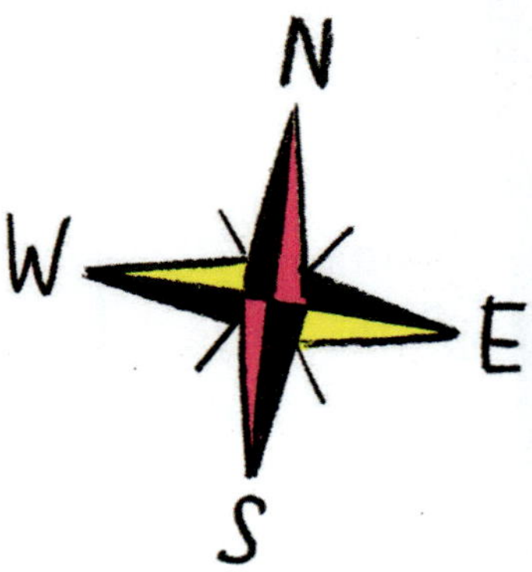

Five – does this make sense? –
I touch, I feel, I smell,
I can even hear and see,
Six, seven, eight, nine as well.

Written by Micro-Climate

Evaluation ▸ Unit 2

1 Get up!

- Order what you would like for breakfast (3 items of food and 2 drinks).

2 How do you spell it?

- Say or sing the alphabet.

- Spell the name of each item.

3 How are you?

- Complete the dialogue:

"– Today, I am ...

– Why?

– Because ..."

4 Let's have some art

- Look at the pictures and describe the people you see.

1 LET'S PLAY IN THE HOUSE

▶ Listen.

▶ Look and listen.

▶ Listen, repeat and point.

1 Listen to the chant

Take the broom
Clean your bedroom
It's not funny, it's not fun!
Tidy your toys
Make your bed
It's not funny, it's not fun!
My bedroom is my bedroom
And as it is, it's much more fun.

2 Let's find out

- Listen.
- Listen and repeat.
- Read the numbers. Any remarks?

eleven (11) twelve (12)
thirteen (13) fourteen (14)
fifteen (15) sixteen (16)
seventeen (17) eighteen (18)
nineteen (19) twenty (20)

3 The world around me

- Where is it? Listen, point and speak.

Remember

- a house, a bathroom, a bedroom, a dining room, a kitchen, a living room, a toilet
- Where is (the table)?
  (The table) is in the dining room.
- 11 (eleven), 12 (twelve), 13 (thirteen), 14 (fourteen), 15 (fifteen), 16 (sixteen), 17 (seventeen), 18 (eighteen), 19 (nineteen), 20 (twenty)

SOUNDS

[r] carrot

- Listen and repeat.

TONGUE TWISTER

Rough and ready Henry
rides home in a hurry.

2 LET'S SET THE TABLE
Unit 3

▶ Listen.

▶ Look and listen.

▶ Listen, repeat and point.

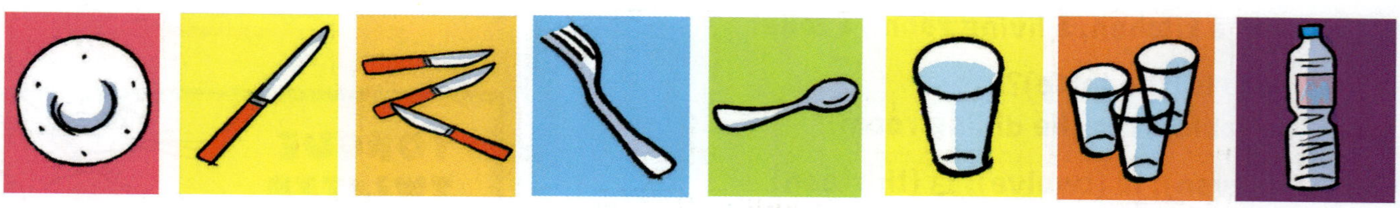

▶ Act and speak (work in pairs).

- What would you like to eat? to drink?

1 Listen to the chant

Five plates, Kate!
Some glasses, Bart!
We need some knives,
Some forks
And some spoons.
Uh huh...
Oh yeaaa!
Let's have a drink!
Cheers!

2 Do it yourself

You invite 3 friends to lunch. Here are some plates and cutlery to set the table.

- What's missing?
- What's not needed?

3 Guessing game

- Knife? fork? spoon? What do I use? Listen and put your hand up.

- Now create your own sentences and play with your friend.

4 Let's find out

- Meat or vegetables? Listen, point and put your hand up.

Remember

Let's set the table.	I am hungry.	I am thirsty.
a bottle	a plate	a knife – knives
a fork	a spoon	a glass – glasses
lunch	meat	vegetables

[ei] Kate or [ai] five

SOUNDS

- Listen and repeat.
- Listen and put your hand up when you hear [ei].

Unit 3

3 LET'S PLAY IN THE GARDEN

▶ Listen.

▶ Look and listen.

▶ Listen, repeat and point.

1 Listen to the chant

Mary Mary
Quite contrary
How does your garden grow?
With silver bells
And cockle shells
And pretty maids
All in a row.

A nursery rhyme.

2 Guessing game

- Look at the sentence.

Richard Of York Gave Battle In Vain.

- Discuss with your teacher.
- Use the sentence to draw and colour a rainbow.

3 Do it yourself

- Look and listen.

- Now listen to your friend and draw.

4 Let's find out: a proverb

- Here is an English proverb.

"A bird in the hand is better than two in the bush".

- What does it mean? Discuss with your teacher and your friends.

Remember

a garden	a bush	a bird
a door	a window	a wall
stairs	upstairs	downstairs
under	next to	in

SOUNDS

[ʌ] Mum or [3:] work

- Listen and repeat.
- Listen and put your hand up when you hear [3:].

WHERE IS IT?

▶ Listen.

▶ Look and listen.

▶ Listen and repeat.

▶ Act and speak.

- Simon says: "stand by me."

1 Listen to the chant

Where is it?
Where is it?
Over and under
Round and round
Where is it?
Where is it?
Not on the bed
Not by the door
Where is it?
Where is it?
Not right, not left
Not here, not there
Not anywhere but here.

2 Do it yourself

Where is it?
Where is it?
...
...
Where is it?
Where is it?
...
...
Not anywhere but here.

3 Let's find out

- Where is it? Look, listen and speak.

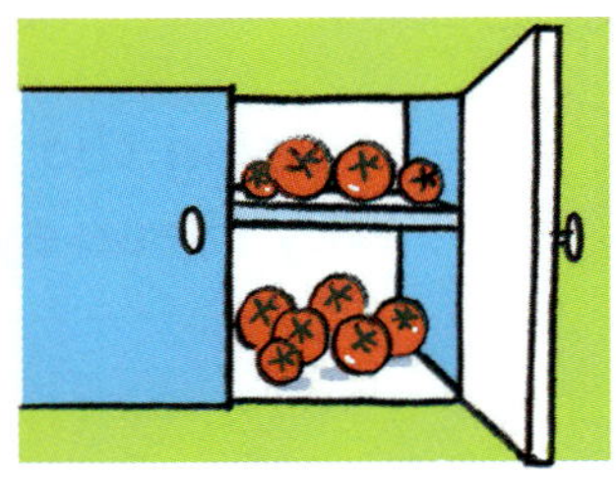

Remember

between	on	in front of
behind	by	right
left	a bed	an armchair
a chair	a cupboard	a settee

[ɒ] dog or [ɔ:] sport

SOUNDS

- Listen and repeat.
- Listen and put your hand up when you hear [ɒ].

Power... action!

1 Rugby and history

Every year, the 6 Nations Rugby Tournament takes place between England, France, Ireland, Italy, Scotland and Wales. The red rose is the symbol of English rugby.

ENGLAND RUGBY

- Look at the following pictures. Each element is used as a rugby symbol by Scotland, Wales or Ireland.

A thistle.

Leeks.

A shamrock.

- Using the Internet, find the right rugby symbol for each country. Why these symbols?

2 A game: I spy

- Look, listen and then play.

3 Let's have some science (work in pairs)

- *Copy and complete the chart with the names of the animals.*

goldfish · snake · rabbit · crab · alligator · blackbird · termite · frog · tiger · spider · salmon · lion · catfish · hippopotamus · snail · giraffe · crocodile · robin · worm · salamander · cricket

Animals without skeleton	Animals with skeleton				

	Fish	Amphibian	Reptile	Bird	Mammal
...	...	...	...	...	...
...	...	...	...	...	...
...	...	...	...	...	...

Workshop (work in groups)

- *Let's make a handprint rainbow.*
- *What you need:*

– white drawing paper;
– some paint of each colour you find in a rainbow;
– your hands!

- *Instructions:*

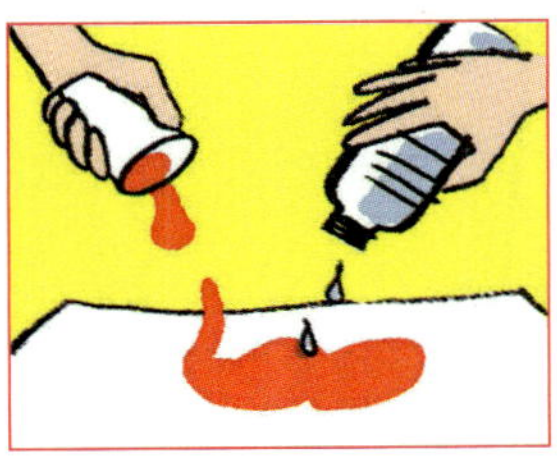

Spread some red paint and a little bit of water on a sheet of paper.

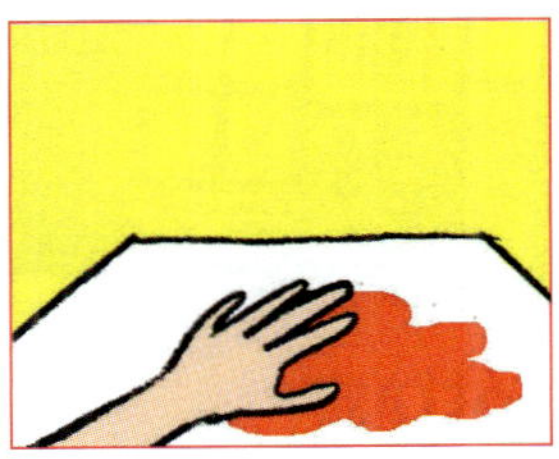

Put your hand on it.

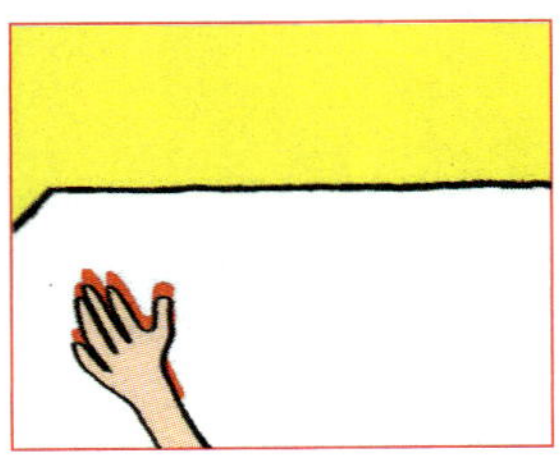

Print your hand on white drawing paper to begin the rainbow.

Then the other children of the group do the same. Continue the same way with the other colours.

CIVILIZATION

A VISIT TO EN

Welcome to English houses in town…

Lots of houses in such a small space! Terrace houses are all attached.

But town houses can also be detached!

An English country cottage. Look at the wonderful thatched roof!

… and in the country!

GLISH HOUSES

Let's have a look at some characteristics

A Tudor style house with beautiful walls.

The door of a Georgian house with its decorated arch.

A Victorian house built with bricks. Look at the bay window!

Every English house has a garden.

Sing a song

Home, sweet home

In pleasures and palaces
Wherever we may go
Be it ever so humble
There's no place like home.

A charm from the skies
Seems to call us there
This charm through the world
Is never met elsewhere.

Home, home,
Home sweet home,
There's no place like home.
Home, home,
Home sweet home,
There's no place like home.

Adapted from a traditional song by Micro-Climate

Evaluation ▸ Unit 3

1 Let's play in the house

- What rooms can you see? Describe.

2 Let's set the table

- Four people are invited to lunch. What do you need?

3 Let's play in the garden

- Describe this garden.
- Say what you would like to have in your garden.

4 Where is it?

- Create four sentences using: in front of – behind – on – under – in – by – between.

Unit 4

1 TELL ME THE WAY

▶ Listen.

▶ Look and listen.

▶ Listen and repeat.

▶ Act and speak (work in pairs).

- Can you tell me the way from the library to the baker's shop?

1 Listen to the chant

Which way, which way?
Tell me the way,
The way to the butcher,
The way to the grocer.

Which way, which way?
Go straight, go down.
Which way, which way?
Turn left, turn right
To get to the grocer,
To get to the butcher.

2 Do it yourself

Which way, which way?
...
The way to ...,
The way to ... .

Which way, which way?
...
Which way, which way?
...
To get to ...,
To get to ... .

3 The world around me

- Listen and point.
- Listen and put your hand up.

Remember

- **Can you tell me the way?**
- **Turn right. / Turn left.**
- **It's straight in front of you.**
- **a baker's shop, a butcher's shop, a grocer's shop, a church, a cinema, a library, a swimming pool**

SOUNDS

[əʊ]
go

- Listen and repeat.

TONGUE TWISTER

Hello, slow Joe! To the grocer run and go.

4 Unit 4 BE CAREFUL ON THE ROAD!

▶ Listen.

▶ Look and listen.

▶ Listen, repeat and point.

1 Listen to the chant

Traffic, traffic,
Beware on the right!
Traffic, traffic,
Beware on the left!
My home town,
My home town,
Cars and buses
Go all around.

2 Guessing game

- Look at the sequence. Any remarks?
- Discuss with your teacher.

3 The world around me

- Describe this picture.

Picadilly Circus, London.

Remember

Be careful!	Cross the road.	Beware on the right / left!
a traffic light	a zebra crossing	a truck
a car	a bus – buses	a taxi

[tʃ] chips or [dʒ] James

SOUNDS

- Listen and repeat.
- Listen and put your hand up when you hear [dʒ].

Power... action!

1 You can count, but can you calculate?

+ PLUS | – MINUS | x MULTIPLIED BY

● Copy and complete.

Fifty plus twenty equals: . . . .

Forty multiplied by two equals: . . . .

Seventy minus thirty equals: . . . .

Forty plus ten equals: . . . .

Thirty plus sixty equals: . . . .

Twenty multiplied by three equals: . . . .

● Listen to your teacher and do it.

10 x 10 = 100 . . . . x . . . . = ... x . . . . = ... x . . . . = ...

2 Geography: let's go to Australia

● Look at the map:

– What's the capital of Australia?
– Name 5 other cities.
– Name 2 seas or oceans.

● In an atlas or on the Internet, find the information to complete the chart, then discuss with your teacher.

	United Kingdom	Australia	France
Area	244 023 km²	. . . .	543 965 km²
Population	59 667 000	. . . .	62 702 000
Capital	London	. . . .	Paris
Population in the capital	7 400 000	. . . .	2 144 700
Language	English	. . . .	French

3 Guessing game

- Look at these drawings and find seven differences.

Workshop

- Look at this Aboriginal painting by Turkey Tolson Tjupurrula. Discuss with your teacher.

- Using the Aboriginal symbols and colours (black, white, brown, red and yellow), create your own composition and describe it.

The Aboriginal symbols

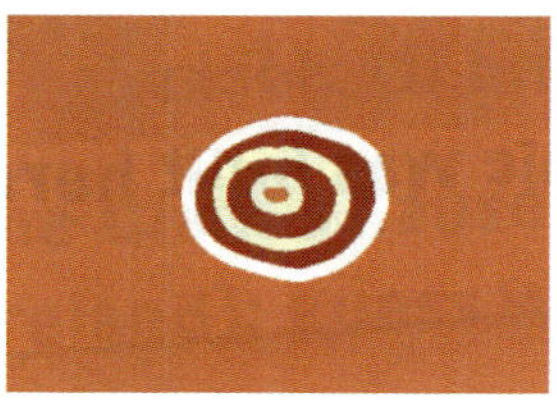

Important site: camp, water...

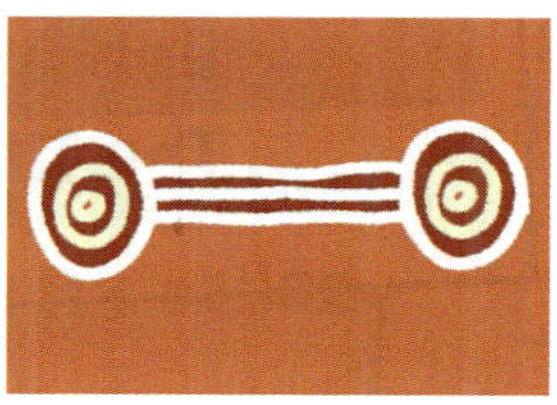

The way between 2 sites.

2 people around a camp.

A river, a snake or a hill.

Sing a song

Nostalgia

My home town, I miss you so
Your streets are in a state
Your factories stand still
Your buses are late
But ask me and I still say you're great.

Oh, oh, I miss my home town
The things I would do with my friends
Oh, oh, I miss being around
I know it sounds funny
I really miss my home town.

I've been to the Red River
Followed it North
And sailed the mighty seas
Seen China, met Cossacks, Aborigines too
Who showed me how to dijeridoo.

Oh, oh, I miss my home town
The things I would do with my friends
Oh, oh, I miss being around
I know it sounds funny
I really miss my home town.

Written by Micro-Climate

Evaluation ▸ Unit 4

1 Tell me the way

- Say how to get from the swimming pool to the cinema.

2 How much is it?

- You go to a toy shop with your parents. Choose what you buy: you have £ 99.50.

3 At the Easter Fair

- You go to the Easter fair with two friends. Prepare the pack lunches.

4 Be careful on the road!

- Act and explain how you cross the road in England.

Power... action!

1 The American flag

- Look at the American flag and describe it.
- Discuss with your teacher the composition of the flag.

2 The travelling game

- Look, listen and then play.

3 Let's have some geography (work in pairs)

- Copy and complete the chart with the geographical vocabulary.

the Atlantic • Canberra • USA • the English Channel • Africa • New York • the North Sea • France • Oceania • Northern Ireland • Cardiff • Scotland • Europe • Washington • Australia • the Pacific • Paris • Asia • the Indian Ocean • Wales • Sydney • Edinburgh • America • the Mediterranean Sea • London • Glasgow • Belfast • England • Nottingham • Lyon

Continents	Countries	Oceans and seas	Capitals	Other cities
...	...	...	...	...
...	...	...	...	...

Workshop

- Look at the picture of Mount Rushmore. Discuss with your teacher.
- Create your own composition including images of some of your heroes in a landscape.

HISTORIC US 66

DISCOVERING

A little bit of history

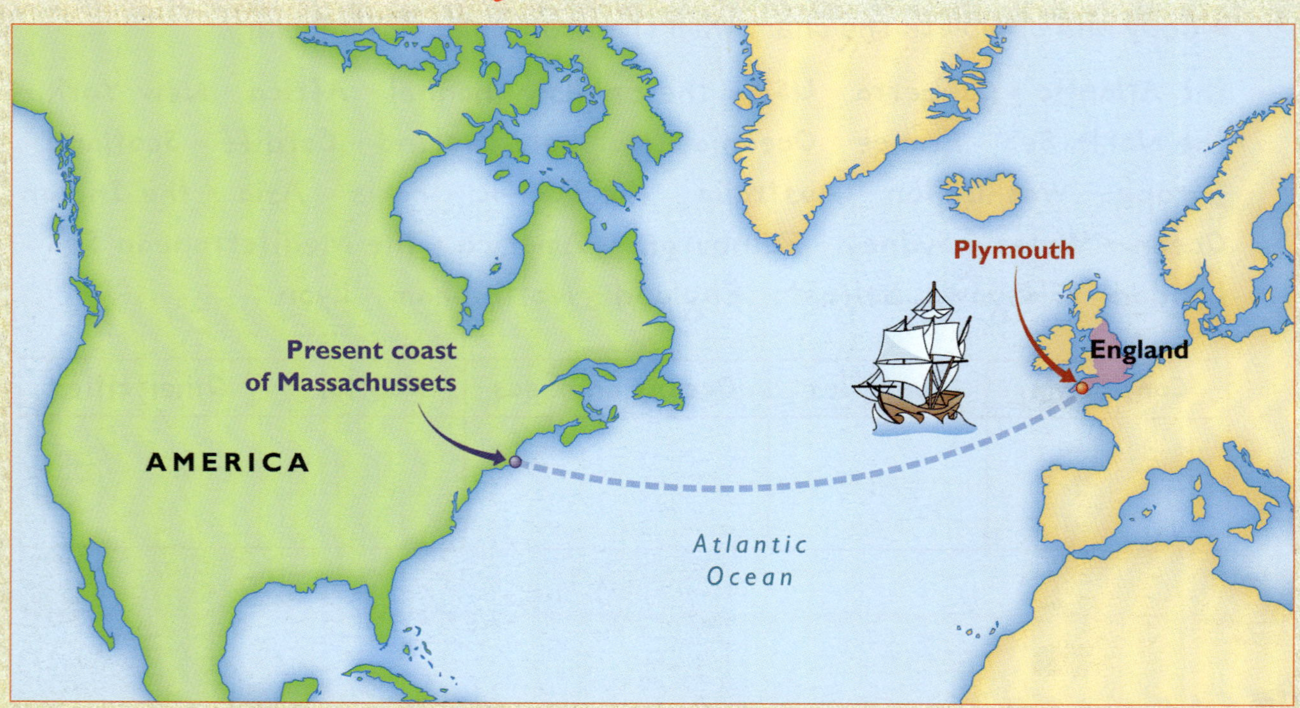

In 1620, some English people (called the Pilgrim fathers) travelled to the new world: America.

The first English pioneers met the local population: indigenous Indians.

The independence of the United States of America is proclaimed in 1776. After a long war, it is recognized by England in 1783.

THE USA

The statue of Liberty welcomes you to New York.

The USA today: a land of diversity

The White House is the home and office of the President of the USA.

The Grand Canyon in Arizona.

Alaska: a very cold and detached state.

Sing a song

Loch Lomond

By your bonnie banks,
And by your bonnie trees,
Where the sun shines bright
on Loch Lomond,
Where me and my true love
Will ever want to be,
On the bonnie, bonnie banks
of Loch Lomond.

Oh! you'll take the high road and
I'll take the low road,
And I'll be in Scotland before you;
But me and my true love
Will never meet again
On the bonnie, bonnie banks
of Loch Lomond.

It was then that we parted
In your shady glen,
On the steep, steep side of Ben
Lomond,
Where in purple light
The Highland hills we view,
And the moon coming out
and glowing.

Adapted from a traditional song by Micro-Climate

Evaluation ▸ Unit 5

1 Holidays

- Name 2 places to spend a holiday and 2 activities you could do there.

2 At the seaside

- Write a postcard to one of your friends.

3 Going to the mountains

- How would you get from Paris to London? Give 3 ways.

4 Flying to the USA

- Complete the sentences.

– I come from Glasgow.
I am ...

– I come from Cardiff.
I am ...

– I come from London.
I am ...

– I come from New York.
I am ...

– I come from Bordeaux.
I am ...

MY ENGLISH WORDS

Greetings and presentations

Good morning
Good afternoon
Good evening
Goodbye
Who are you?
I am (David). / I'm (David).
How old are you?
I am nine years old.
How old is she / he?
She / He is ten.
When is your birthday?
My birthday is in June.
Where do you come from?
I come from (London).
I live in (London).
I am American.
I am English.
I am French.
I am Scottish.
I am Welsh.

Pets

a cat
a dog
a goldfish
a guinea pig
a hamster
a mouse
a rabbit

Family

What's your brother's name?
aunt(y)
brother
cousin
father
grandma
grandpa
mother
sister
uncle

Clothes

What shall I put on?
What shall I wear?
boots
a coat
a hat
jeans
a jumper
a pullover
pyjamas
shoes
socks
a tee-shirt

School

the alphabet
felt markers
a pen
a pencil
a pencil case
a rubber
a ruler
a school bag
school things
scissors

Feelings and sensations

How are you?
What's up?
Not so good!
I'm happy / sad / scared / tired / worried
Why? Because …
I like (maths).
I prefer (history).
I'm (not) good at (maths).

Colours

black
blue
green
indigo
orange
pink

red
violet
white
yellow

Description

beautiful
big
fat
old
slim
small
tall
young

The house

an armchair
a bathroom
a bed
a bedroom
a chair
a cupboard
a dining room
a door
a kitchen
a living room
a settee
stairs
a toilet
a wall
a window

The table

Let's set the table.
a bottle
a fork
a glass – glasses
a knife – knives
a plate
a spoon

Food and drinks

I am hungry.
I am thirsty.
an apple pie

MY ENGLISH WORDS

bacon
beans
breakfast
butter
cereals
chocolate
eggs
fruit juice
ham
jam
lemonade
lunch
meat
milk
pickles
a sandwich
sausage
sweet corn
tea
toast
tuna
vegetables
water

Nature

a bird
a bush
a garden
a lake
a robin
a rose
a snail
a stream
a worm

Location

Where is it?
It's on the table.
Where is (the table)?
(The table) is in the (dining room).
behind
between
by
downstairs
in
left
next to
on
right
(straight) in front of
under
upstairs

In town

a baker's shop
a butcher's shop
a church
a cinema
a grocer's shop
a library
a swimming pool

Numbers

Count up to a hundred.
How much is it?
It's 84 pence / pounds.
11 eleven
12 twelve
13 thirteen
14 fourteen
15 fifteen
16 sixteen
17 seventeen
18 eighteen
19 nineteen
20 twenty
30 thirty
40 forty
50 fifty
60 sixty
70 seventy
80 eighty
90 ninety
100 (a) hundred

Easter time

Happy Easter!
Easter bonnets
Easter bunnies
Easter eggs
hot cross buns

Road and means of transport

Beware on the right / left!
Cross the road.
How do you get to (England)?
How do you get from (London) to (Brighton)?
I get to (Spain) by plane.
a bicycle
a bus – buses
a car
a coach
a plane
a taxi
a traffic light
a train
a truck
a zebra crossing

Holidays

Where are you going?
I am going surfing.
I'm going mountain trekking.
I'm having a great time!
... building sand castles
... playing beach volleyball.
... sailing.
... sleeping in the sun.
... staying home.
... swimming in the sea.
... touring (the USA).
the countryside
the mail
the mountains
a postcard
the postman
the seaside
the summer holidays

MY ENGLISH WORDS

Common sentences

Get up!
Hurry up!
You are / You're late!
Who is this?
He is / He's tall.
She is / She's small.
What would you like?

I would like (milk).
Have you got (a pen)?
Yes, I have.
No, I haven't.
I have got (a pencil).
I haven't got (a pencil).
Why? Because ...
Can you tell me the way?
Turn right. / Turn left.

How much is it?
It's 84 (pounds) 32 pence.
Thank you!
You're welcome.
How many (eggs) are there?
There is (one egg).
There are (three eggs).
Be careful!

Crédits texte

L'activité **Workshop** de la page 31 (fabrication du chapeau de *Robin Hood*) a été rédigée d'après un texte publié sur le site **www.teteamodeler.com** (fiche n° 458), avec l'aimable autorisation de Fanny Lacroix, créatrice du site.

Crédits photographiques

p. 11 : hippopotame, © Tony Heald / NPL / Jacana ; chiot berger australien, © Shanz Ulrike / Jacana ; tigre du Bengale, © Adam Jones / Imagestate / GHFP ; souris blanche, © Lemoine Elizabeth / Jacana. – **p. 18 :** Guy Fawkes (lithographie coloriée extraite de *Peeps into the past*, publiée vers 1900), © Trelleek / The Bridgeman Art Library / Getty Images ; Guy Fawkes devant le roi James (1869-70, Harrogate Museums and Art Gallery, North Yorkshire, UK), © Sir John Gilbert / The Bridgeman Art Library / Getty Images. – **p. 19 :** feux d'artifices pour la Guy Fawkes'night, © Michael St. Maur Sheil / Corbis ; défilé de la Guy Fawkes'night, © Toby Melville / Reuters / Corbis ; feux d'artifices pour la Guy Fawkes'night, © Adrian Caroll, Eye Ubiquitous / Corbis. – **p. 29 :** tableau de Sir Edwin Landseer, © National Gallery, London, UK / The Bridgeman Art Library ; tableau de Thomas Gainsborough, © Christie's Images / The Bridgeman Art Library – **p. 30 :** sculpture de Niki de Saint-Phalle, © Benoît Decout / Réa – **p. 32 :** portrait de Robin des bois (étiquette de cigares, vers 1900), © Selva / Leemage ; Robin des bois et ses amis (lithographie coloriée, vers 1850), © akg-images. – **p. 33 :** attaque (étiquette de cigares, vers 1900), © Selva / Leemage ; sac de pièces, © Heritage Images / Leemage ; image extraite du dessin animé « Robin des bois », © Disney, par autorisation spéciale de TWDCF et © akg-images ; Kevin Costner dans le film « Robin des bois, prince des voleurs », © Rue des Archives / CSFF. – **p. 44 :** chardon, © Geoff du Feu / Imagestate / GHFP ; poireaux, © Jonathan Kantor / The Image Bank / Getty Images ; trèfle, © Neil Letcher et Matthew Ward / Dorling Kindersley / Getty Images. – **p. 46 :** heurtoir de porte, © Ric Ergenbright / Corbis ; maisons victoriennes en rang, © Phillipa Lewis / Edifice / Corbis ; maison anglaise avec les fenêtres illuminées, © David Oliver / Taxi / Getty Images ; maison de campagne anglaise, © TSI Pictures / Stone / Getty Images. – **p. 47 :** maison style Tudor © Tony Craddock / Stone / Getty Images ; porte d'une maison georgienne, © Philipa Lewis / Edifice / Corbis ; entrée d'une maison victorienne, © Elizabeth Whiting & Associates / Corbis ; vue aérienne de Londres, © Martin Barraud / Photographer's choice / Getty Images. – **p. 57 :** vue aérienne de Picadilly Circus (Londres), © Bettmann / Corbis. – **p. 59 :** peinture aborigène traditionnelle de Turkey Tolson Tjupurrula, © The estate of the artist licensed by Aboriginal Artists Agency, Sydney 2006 et © Penny Tweedie / Corbis. – **p. 60 :** bords de la Tamise, © Bruno Perousse / Hoa-Qui ; château de Cardiff, © Julie Houck / Corbis ; le « Royal Mile » à Édimbourg, © Rick Lew / The Image Bank / Getty Images ; vue aérienne du port de Belfast, © Altitude / Yann Arthus-Bertrand. – **p. 61 :** Loch Ness (Écosse), © Eitan Simanor / Hoa-Qui ; Blaenavon (Pays de Galles), © The Heritage Trail Image Library ; the Giant's Causeway, © John Lawrence / The Image Bank / Getty Images ; plage de Brighton, © Paul Seheult / Eye Ubiquitous / Corbis. – **p. 69 :** Derwent Water, © Brian Lawrence / Imagestate / GHFP. – **p. 73 :** le mont Rushmore, © Johnny Stockshooter / Hoa-Qui. – **p. 74 :** panneau de la route 66, © Jeff Greenberg / Age Fotostock / Hoa-Qui ; signature de la Déclaration d'indépendance du 4 juillet 1776 (tableau de John Trumbull), © Capitol Collection, Washington, USA / The Bridgeman Art Library ; indien iroquois (gravure), © Rue des Archives / The Granger collection N.Y.C. – **p. 75 :** vue aérienne de la statue de la Liberté, © A & L Sinibaldi / Stone / Getty Images ; la Maison blanche, © Dennis O'Clair / Stone / Getty Images ; Grand Canyon, © Sylvain Grandadam / Hoa-Qui ; glacier John Hopkins, © Walter Bibikow / Age Fotostock / Hoa-Qui.

Artiste représenté par l'ADAGP : © ADAGP, Paris 2007 : sculpture de Niki de Saint-Phalle dans la cour de la Banque générale du Luxembourg, p. 30.

Achevé d'imprimer en Italie par Bona - Dépôt légal : 09/2009 - Edition 04 - Collection n° 70 11/7353/3